NASIR PERSEVERES

Illustrated by: Mary Ibeh

Nasir Hopewell: Nasir Hopewell is an African American boy age 10 who lived with both parents until they were divorced; he now lives in an urban neighborhood with his mother. Nasir enjoys helping others. He is also an entrepreneurial spirit. He created his own multimedia company called Nasir's Vision LLC by saving up his money along with a few of his friends to buy necessary equipment, software and other materials. He is also a young investor in the company Dream Plan Execute LLC a personal and entrepreneurial development company.

Nasir Feeds the Homesless

Nasir loves to help others
So he saved up money from his mother
He took the money and went to the store
It didn't matter that he was considered poor
He had a lot to give because he was healthy
Helping other people was how he felt wealthy
His love for humanity was one of the strongest
He took the food from the store to feed the homeless

Nasir Unites the People

All of the kids are on stage

Some are singing and dancing and others afraid

They're having a talent show for children

There are over 1,000 people in the building

Some of the parents are crying in need
of tissues

But Nasir wants to talk about real life issues

He said "There's so much hate that we face

And together we must save the human race

Nasir Bounces Back

Nasir is failing his course

His parents are getting a divorce

He's beginning to feel unlucky

So he went to the pet store and bought a puppy

He named the puppy Bear Max

He's a Rottweiler who helps him relax

He decided to write himself a letter

That read "from this day I will do better"

He was motivated to set that kind of goal

In the following year he made the honor roll

Nasir Helps His Friend

Nasir has a friend named Sophia Sanders

Sophia has questions but she needs answers

Sophia is an artist who's planning an art show

But she doesn't know where to start though

She has to invite people and promote her art

Nasir promised that he would help her start

Nasir Finds Inspiration

Nasir's Grandmother just passed away

He has to give a presentation today

He knows that she would want him to get an A

But today he's just not feeling okay

He thought about how proud it would make her

Overcoming obstacles was in his nature

He researched all of the needed information

He found inspiration and gave a stellar
presentation

Nasir Creates Jobs

Nasir noticed a need for jobs in his community

And how it would make people happier and
create unity

He decided to meet up with 2 of his friends

To figure out a means to achieve those ends

He received a loan from his mentor Mr. Sanders

To build a multimedia company for better
community answers

He hired black professionals to help build
his team

Creating jobs for his community was
Nasir's dream

Nasir and Bear Max Go Running

Today is a very beautiful day

And Bear Max wants to go out and play

Nasir is motivated about taking him for a run

He really loves to exercise in the sun

The steep hills can be quite a high climb

But Nasir and Bear Max had a fine time

<u>Nasir's Vision</u>

Nasir's new company is doing really well

His friends are proud of him and it's easy to tell

They said "It's great to see Nasir's vision come to fruition"

He works really hard and barely watches television

He built this business to help his community

To create jobs and really bring unity

His friends helped him without any hesitation

And now they're having a big celebration

<u>*Nasir Volunteers*</u>

Nasir created a program to shovel snow

He spread the word to let everyone know

His program will serve the elderly

By matching them with youth who will shovel for free

The program really depends on volunteers

Nasir's program received a lot of cheers

Nasir Supports Flint

Nasir decided to support Flint

So he organized a big event

He set it up under a huge tent

To collect bottled water to be sent

A few neighborhood men volunteered

To rent trucks and drive them there

He wanted to put smiles on all those
innocent faces

So they were able to collect 1,000 cases

Nasir Meets the Mayor

Nasir has inspired the mayor

So they met to discuss what was in the air

The mayor wants to push volunteerism

When they met there was a clear rhythm

Although Nasir was only the tender age of 10

The Mayor depended on Nasir to help him begin

They sat down and the mayor made the
problem clear

The city wants to encourage more people to
volunteer

Entrepreneur is the Word

"Being creative is the key

And ownership is what makes us free"

Nasir gave a big speech to his peers

None of them were older than him by more than
5 years

The students were inspired by his speech

One of the kids jumped up and yelled "Preach"

This confused an older man in the front who
asked "what is this"

Nasir replied "this is inspiring kids to start
their own business"

Joshua "Ridock King" Keller is a book author, poet, music artist, and entrepreneur from Philadelphia, PA.

The concept behind the creation of "Nasir Persevere's" was the need to inspire children and youth to dream big and pursue their dreams. It was also designed to help motivate parents, teachers, and community leaders to get children more involved within the community. The idea is that every child is born with a gift and it is our job to help them identify that gift so that they are better prepared to walk in their purpose. This book also encourages children and youth to persevere through life's challenges and to remain motivated to set goals and reach those goals. "Nasir Persevere's" is a must-read book for children, youth, parents, teachers, and leaders across the globe.